JAPANESE SOCIETY

Published under the auspices of
The Center for Japanese and Korean Studies
University of California, Berkeley

The Center for Japanese and Korean Studies of the University of California is a unit of the Institute of International Studies. It is the unifying organization for faculty members and students interested in Japan and Korea, bringing together scholars from many disciplines.

The Center's major aims are the development and support of research and language study. As part of this program the Center sponsors a publication series of books concerned with Japan and Korea. Manuscripts are considered from all campuses of the University of California as well as from any other individuals and institutions doing research in these areas.

PUBLICATIONS OF THE CENTER FOR JAPANESE AND
KOREAN STUDIES

CHONG-SIK LEE
The Politics of Korean Nationalism. 1963

SADAKO N. OGATA
Defiance in Manchuria: The Making of Japanese Foreign Policy, 1931–1932.
1964

R. P. DORE
Education in Tokugawa Japan. 1964

JAMES T. ARAKI
The Ballad-Drama of Medieval Japan. 1964

MASAKAZU IWATA
Okubo Toshimichi: The Bismarck of Japan. 1964

FRANK O. MILLER
Minobe Tatsukichi: Interpreter of Constitutionalism in Japan. 1965

MICHAEL COOPER, S.J.
*They Came to Japan: An Anthology of European Reports on Japan,
1543–1640.* 1965

GEORGE DE VOS AND HIROSHI WAGATSUMA
Japan's Invisible Race. 1966

RYUTARO KOMIYA, Ed.
Translated from the Japanese by Robert S. Ozaki
Postwar Economic Growth in Japan. 1966

ROBERT A. SCALAPINO
The Japanese Communist Movement, 1920–1966. 1967

SOON SUNG CHO
Korea in World Politics, 1940–1950: An Evaluation of American Responsibility. 1967

KOZO YAMAMURA
Economic Policy in Postwar Japan: Growth versus Economic Democracy.
1967

C. I. EUGENE KIM AND HAN-KYO KIM
Korea and the Politics of Imperialism, 1876–1910. 1967

EARL MINER, Trans.
Japanese Poetic Diaries. 1969

DONALD C. HELLMANN
Japanese Foreign Policy and Domestic Politics. 1969

IRWIN SCHEINER
Christian Converts and Social Protest in Meiji Japan. 1970

H. D. HAROOTUNIAN
*Toward Restoration: The Growth of Political Consciousness in Tokugawa
Thought.* 1970

CONTENTS

PREFACE

This short work presents a configuration of the important elements to be found in contemporary Japanese social life, and attempts to shed new light on Japanese society. I deal with my own society as a social anthropologist using some of the methods which I am accustomed to applying in examining any other society. However, its form is not that of a scientific thesis (as may be seen at once from the absence of a bibliography; I have also refrained from quoting any statistical figures or precise data directly obtained from field surveys).

In this book I have tried to construct a structural image of Japanese society, synthesizing the major distinguishing features to be found in Japanese life. I have drawn evidence almost at random from a number of different types of community to be found in Japan today – industrial enterprises, government organizations, educational institutions, intellectual groups, religious communities, political parties, village communities, individual households and so on. Throughout my investigation of groups in such varied fields, I have concentrated my analysis on individual behaviour and interpersonal relations which provide the base of both the group organization and the structural tendencies dominating in the development of a group.

It may appear to some that my statements in this book are in some respects exaggerated or over-generalized; such critics might raise objections based on the observations that they themselves happen to have made. Others might object that my examples are not backed by precise or detailed data. Certainly this book does not cover the entire range of social phenomena in Japanese life, nor does it pretend to offer accurate data relevant to a particular community. This is not a description of Japanese society or culture *or* the Japanese people, nor an explanation of limited phenomena such as the urbanization or modernization of Japan. Rather, it is my intention that this book will offer a key (a source of intelligence and insight) to an understanding of Japanese society, and those features which are specific to it and which distinguish it from other complex societies. I have used wide-ranging suggestive evidence as material to illustrate the crucial aspects of Japanese life, for the understanding of the structural core of Japanese society rather as an artist uses his colours. I had a distinct advantage in handling these colours, for they are colours in which I was born and among which I grew up; I know their delicate shades and effects. In handling these colours, I did not employ any known sociological method and theory. Instead, I have used anything available which seemed to be effective in bringing out the core of the subject matter. This is an approach which might be closer to that of the social anthropologist than to that of the conventional sociologist.

The theoretical basis of the present work was originally established in my earlier study, *Kinship and Economic Organization in Rural Japan* (Athlone Press, London, 1967). This developed out of my own field work, including detailed monographs by others, in villages in Japan and, as soon as that research was completed, I was greatly tempted to test further, in modern society, the ideas which had emerged from my examination of a rather traditional rural society. In my view, the traditional social structure of a complex society, such as Japan, China or India, seems to persist and endure in spite of great modern changes. Hence, a further and wider exploration of my ideas, as attempted in this book, was called for in order to strengthen the theoretical basis of my earlier study.

Some of the distinguishing aspects of Japanese society which I treat in this book are not exactly new to Japanese and western observers and may be familiar from discussions in previous writings on Japan. However, my *interpretations* are different and the way in which I *synthesize* these aspects is new. Most of the sociological studies of contemporary Japan have been concerned primarily with its changing aspects, pointing to the 'traditional' and 'modern' elements as representing different or opposing qualities. The hey-day of this kind of approach came during the American occupation and in the immediately subsequent years, when it was the standpoint adopted by both Japanese and American social scientists. The tendency towards such an approach is still prevalent; it is their thesis that any phenomena which seem peculiar to Japan, not having been found in western society, can be labelled as 'feudal' or 'pre-modern' elements, and are to be regarded as contradictory or obstructive to modernization. Underneath such views, it seems that there lurks a kind of correlative and syllogistic view of social evolution: when it is completely modernized Japanese society will or should become the same as that of the west. The proponents of such views are interested either in uprooting feudal elements or in discovering and noting modern elements which are comparable to those of the west. The fabric of Japanese society has thus been made to appear to be torn into pieces of two kinds. But in fact it remains as one well-integrated entity. In my view, the 'traditional' is one aspect (not element) of the same social body which also has 'modern' features. I am more interested in the truly basic components and their potentiality in the society – in other words, in social persistence.

The persistence of social structure can be seen clearly in the modes of personal social relation which determine the probable variability of group organization in changing circumstances. This persistence reveals the basic value orientation inherent in society, and is the driving force of the development of society. Social tenacity is dependent largely on the degree of integration and the time span of the history of a society. In Japan, India, China and elsewhere, rich and well-integrated economic and social development occurred during the pre-modern period, comparable to the 'post-feudal' era in European history and helped create a unique institutionalization of social ideals. Values that crystallized into definite form during the course of pre-modern history are deeply rooted and aid or hinder, as the case may be, the process of modernization. To explore these values in terms of their effects on social structure appears to me to be a fascinating subject for the social sciences. In this light, I think Japan presents a rich field for the development of a theory of social structure.

I approach this issue through a structural analysis, not a cultural or historical explanation. The working of what I call the *vertical principle* in Japanese society is the theme of this book. In my view, the most characteristic feature of Japanese social organization arises from the single bond in social relationships: an individual or a group has always one single distinctive relation to the other. The working of this kind of relationship meets the unique structure of Japanese society as a whole, which contrasts to that of caste or class societies. And the Japanese values are accordingly manifested. Some of my Japanese readers might feel repelled in the face of some parts of my discussion; where I expose certain Japanese weaknesses they might even feel considerable distaste. I do this, however, not because of a hyper-critical view of the Japanese or Japanese life but because I intend to be as objective as possible in this analysis of the society to which I belong. I myself take these weaknesses for granted as elements which constitute part of the entire body which also has its great strengths.

Finally, I wish to express my profound thanks to Professor Ernest Gellner, whose very stimulating and detailed comments as editor helped me a great deal in completing the final version of the manuscript.* I am greatly indebted to Professor Geoffrey Bownas, who kindly undertook the difficult task of correcting my English. I was fascinated by the way he found it possible to make my manuscript so much more readable without altering even a minor point in the flow of my discussion.

C. N.

---

* My theory, which forms the basis of the discussion of this book, was first presented in the form of a short essay in Japanese: *Nihonteki shakai-kōzō no hakken* ('A new light on Japanese social structure'), *Chuōkōron*, May 1964, pp. 48–85. English and German translations of this essay were published as follows: 'Towards a Theory of Japanese Social Structure' (translated by W. H. Newell and his students, the International Christian University, Tokyo) in *The Economic Weekly*, Bombay, February 1965, Volume 17, pp. 197–215; 'Entdecking der Japanischen Gesellschaftsstruktur' (translated by J. Koschel) in *Kagami, Japanischer Zeitschriftenspiegel* III, Band 2, Heft 1965, Deutsche Gesellschaft für Natür and Völkerkund Ostasiens, Tokyo, Institut für Asienkunde, Hamburg, pp. 71–104; 'A Theory on the Japanese Social Structure – An Analysis of Contemporary Japanese Society' (translated by Joseph Goedertier), in *The Japan Missionary Bulletin*, XXI, 6 & 8, 1967, pp. 373–8, 386, 496–502. The first draft

of my English version was prepared at the Institute of Advanced Projects, East–West Center, Hawaii, in 1964, when I was invited as a senior specialist. I am grateful for the comments of colleagues there, the collaboration of the staff of the Institute and in particular, the very able services of Mrs Grace Merritt.

The present manuscript has been greatly enriched and improved by the many helpful comments and materials I have received from various sectors subsequently. I have received encouraging comments from my colleagues in social anthropology, particularly Professors Sol Tax, Fred Eggan, Raymond Firth, and Drs Edmund Leach and W. H. Newell, to whom I am very grateful. The original essay was revised and published in Japan under the title: *Tate-shakai no ningen-kankei – Tanitsu-shakai no riron* ('Personal Relations in a Vertical Society – A Theory of Homogeneous Society'), Kōdansha, Tokyo, 1967. I owe a great deal to audiences in academic and business institutions whose comments at meetings to discuss the Japanese edition have been incorporated in this English version.

GROUP FORMATION

basic contrasting criteria or concepts,
ne, which are newly formulated by myself,
nost effective in the analysis of Japanese
ith other societies. These two terms, with
he distinction is employed, might lead the
customary European thought, but they are
erent way and the resemblance is merely

iew, groups may be identified by applying the
based on the individual's common *attribute*, the
al position in a given *frame*. I use *frame* as a
ith a particular significance as opposed to the
bute, which, again, is used specifically and in a
han it normally carries. *Frame* may be a locality, an
a particular relationship which binds a set of indi-
one group: in all cases it indicates a criterion which
lary and gives a common basis to a set of individuals
cated or involved in it. In fact, my term *frame* is the
anslation of the Japanese *ba*, the concept from which I
evolved my theory, but for which it is hard to find the
nglish counterpart. *Ba* means 'location', but the normal
f the term connotes a special base on which something is
according to a given purpose. The term *ba* is also used in
cs for 'field' in English.
et me indicate how these two technical terms can be applied

I

to various actual contexts. Attribute may mean, for instan
a member of a definite descent group or caste. In contra
a member of X village expresses the commonality o
Attribute may be acquired not only by birth but by achie
Frame is more circumstantial. These criteria serve to ide
individuals in a certain group, which can then in its
classified within the whole society, even though the group
may not have a particular function of its own as a collectiv
Classifications such as landlord and tenant are based on at
while such a unit as a landlord and his tenants is a group
by situational position. Taking industry as an example,
operator' or 'executive' refers to attribute, but 'the membe
Company' refers to frame. In the same way, 'professor',
clerk' and 'student' are attributes, whereas 'men of Z Univ
is a frame.

In any society, individuals are gathered into social grou
social strata on the bases of attributes and frame. There
be some cases where the two factors coincide in the formatio
group, but usually they overlap each other, with indivi
belonging to different groups at the same time. The pri
concern in this discussion is the relative degree of function of
criterion. There are some cases where either the attribute o
frame factor functions alone, and some where the two are mut
competitive. The way in which the factors are commonly weig
bears a close reciprocal relationship to the values which dev
in the social consciousness of the people in the society. For
ample, the group consciousness of the Japanese depends consi
ably on this immediate social context, frame, whereas in Ind
lies in attribute (most symbolically expressed in caste, whic
fundamentally a social group based on the ideology of occupat
and kinship). On this point, perhaps, the societies of Japan a
India show the sharpest contrast, as will be discussed later
greater detail.

The ready tendency of the Japanese to stress situational positi
in a particular frame, rather than universal attribute, can be se
in the following example: when a Japanese 'faces the outsid
(confronts another person) and affixes some position to hims

socially he is inclined to give precedence to institution over kind of occupation. Rather than saying, 'I am a type-setter' or 'I am a filing clerk', he is likely to say, 'I am from B Publishing Group' or 'I belong to S Company'. Much depends on context, of course, but where a choice exists, he will use this latter form. (I will discuss later the more significant implications for Japanese social life indicated by this preference.) The listener would rather hear first about the connection with B Publishing Group or S Company; that he is a journalist or printer, engineer or office worker is of secondary importance. When a man says he is from X Television one may imagine him to be a producer or cameraman, though he may in fact be a chauffeur. (The universal business suit makes it hard to judge by appearances.) In group identification, a frame such as a 'company' or 'association' is of primary importance; the attribute of the individual is a secondary matter. The same tendency is to be found among intellectuals: among university graduates, what matters most, and functions the strongest socially, is not whether a man holds or does not hold a PhD but rather from which university he graduated. Thus the criterion by which Japanese classify individuals socially tends to be that of particular institution, rather than of universal attribute. Such group consciousness and orientation fosters the strength of an institution, and the institutional unit (such as school or company) is in fact the basis of Japanese social organization, as will be discussed extensively in Chapter Three.

The manner in which this group consciousness works is also revealed in the way the Japanese uses the expression *uchi* (my house) to mean the place of work, organization, office or school to which he belongs; and *otaku* (your house) to mean a second person's place of work and so on. The term *kaisha* symbolizes the expression of group consciousness. *Kaisha* does not mean that individuals are bound by contractual relationships into a corporate enterprise, while still thinking of themselves as separate entities; rather, *kaisha* is 'my' or 'our' company, the community to which one belongs primarily, and which is all-important in one's life. Thus in most cases the company provides the whole social existence of a person, and has authority over all aspects of his life; he is

3

deeply emotionally involved in the association.* That Company A belongs not to its shareholders, but rather belongs to 'us', is the sort of reasoning involved here, which is carried to such a point that even the modern legal arrangement must compromise in face of this strong native orientation. I would not wish to deny that in other societies an employee may have a kind of emotional attachment to the company or his employer; what distinguishes this relation in Japan is the exceedingly high degree of this emotional involvement. It is openly and frequently expressed in speech and behaviour in public as well as in private, and such expressions always receive social and moral appreciation and approbation.

The essence of this firmly rooted, latent group consciousness in Japanese society is expressed in the traditional and ubiquitous concept of *ie*, the household, a concept which penetrates every nook and cranny of Japanese society. The Japanese usage *uchi-no* referring to one's work place indeed derives from the basic concept of *ie*. The term *ie* also has implications beyond those to be found in the English words 'household' or 'family'.

The concept of *ie*, in the guise of the term 'family system', has been the subject of lengthy dispute and discussion by Japanese legal scholars and sociologists. The general consensus is that, as a consequence of modernization, particularly because of the new post-war civil code, the *ie* institution is dying. In this ideological approach the *ie* is regarded as being linked particularly with feudal moral precepts; its use as a fundamental unit of social structure has not been fully explored.

In my view, the most basic element of the *ie* institution is not that form whereby the eldest son and his wife live together with the old parents, nor an authority-structure in which the household head holds the power and so on. Rather, the *ie* is a corporate residential group and, in the case of agriculture or other similar enterprises, *ie* is a managing body. The *ie* comprises household members (in most cases the family members of the household head, but

* I find it difficult to choose an English equivalent for *kaisha*: though 'company' or 'enterprise' correspond etymologically, they do not have the social implications that the word *kaisha* has for a Japanese.

4

others in addition to family members may be included), who thus make up the units of a distinguishable social group. In other words, the *ie* is a social group constructed on the basis of an established frame of residence and often of management organization. What is important here is that the human relationships within this household group are thought of as more important than all other human relationships. Thus the wife and daughter-in-law who have come from outside have incomparably greater importance than one's own sisters and daughters, who have married and gone into other households. A brother, when he has built a separate house, is thought of as belonging to another unit or household; on the other hand, the son-in-law, who was once a complete outsider, takes the position of a household member and becomes more important than the brother living in another household. This is remarkably different from societies such as that of India, where the weighty factor of sibling relationship (a relationship based on commonality of attribute, that of being born of the same parents) continues paramount until death, regardless of residential circumstances; theoretically, the stronger the factor of sibling relationship, the weaker the social independence of a household (as a residence unit). (It goes without saying, of course, that customs such as the adopted son-in-law system prevalent in Japan are non-existent in Hindu society. The same is true of Europe.) These facts support the theory that group-forming criteria based on functioning by attribute oppose group-forming criteria based on functioning by frame.

Naturally, the function of forming groups on the basis of the element of the frame, as demonstrated in the formation of the household, involves the possibility of including members with a differing attribute, and at the same time expelling a member who has the same attribute. This is a regular occurrence, particularly among traditional agricultural and merchant households. Not only may outsiders with not the remotest kinship tie be invited to be heirs and successors but servants and clerks are usually incorporated as members of the household and treated as family members by the head of the household. This inclusion must be accepted without reservation to ensure that when a clerk is married to the daughter of the household and becomes an adopted son-in-law the household succession will continue without disruption.

Such a principle contributes to the weakening of kinship ties. Kinship, the core of which lies in the sibling relation, is a criterion based on attribute. Japan gives less weight to kinship than do other societies even England and America; in fact, the function of kinship is comparatively weak outside the household. The saying 'the sibling is the beginning of the stranger' accurately reflects Japanese ideas on kinship. A married sibling who lives in another household is considered a kind of outsider. Towards such kin, duties and obligations are limited to the level of the seasonal exchange of greetings and presents, attendance at wedding and funeral ceremonies and the minimum help in case of accident or poverty. There are often instances where siblings differ widely in social and economic status; the elder brother may be the mayor, while his younger brother is a postman in the same city; or a brother might be a lawyer or businessman, while his widowed sister works as a domestic servant in another household. The wealthy brother normally does not help the poor brother or sister, who has set up a separate household, as long as the latter can somehow support his or her existence; by the same token, the latter will not dare to ask for help until the last grain of rice has gone. Society takes this for granted, for it gives prime importance to the individual household rather than to the kin group as a whole.

This is indeed radically different from the attitudes to kin found in India and other south east Asian countries, where individual wealth tends to be distributed among relatives; here the kin group as a whole takes precedence over the individual household and nepotism plays an important role. I have been surprised to discover that even in England and America, brothers and sisters meet much more frequently than is required by Japanese standards, and that there exists such a high degree of attachment to kinfolk. Christmas is one of the great occasions when these kinfolk gather together; New Year's Day is Japan's equivalent to the western Christmas, everyone busy with preparations for visits from subordinate staff, and then, in turn, calling on superiors. There is little time and scope to spare for collateral kin – married brothers, sisters, cousins, uncles and aunts and so on – though parents and grandparents will certainly be visited if they do not live in the same house. Even in rural areas, people say, 'One's neighbour is of more importance than one's relatives' or 'You can carry on your life without cousins, but not without your neighbours'.

The kinship which is normally regarded as the primary and basic human attachment seems to be compensated in Japan by a personalized relation to a corporate group based on work, in which the major aspects of social and economic life are involved. Here again we meet the vitally important unit in Japanese society of the corporate group based on frame. In my view, this is the basic principle on which Japanese society is built.

To sum up, the principles of Japanese social group structure can be seen clearly portrayed in the household structure. The concept of this traditional household institution, *ie*, still persists in the various group identities which are termed *uchi*, a colloquial form of *ie*. These facts demonstrate that the formation of social groups on the basis of fixed frames remains characteristic of Japanese social structure.

Among groups larger than the household, there is that described by the medieval concept, *ichizoku-rōtō* (one family group and its retainers). The idea of group structure as revealed in this expression is an excellent example of the frame-based social group. This is indeed the concept of one household, in which family members and retainers are not separated but form an integrated corporate group. There are often marriage ties between the two sides of this corporate group, and all lines of distinction between them become blurred. The relationship is the same as that between family members and clerks or servants in a household. This is a theoretical antithesis to a group formed exclusively on lineage or kin.

The equivalent in modern society of *ie* and *ichizokurōtō* is a group such as 'One Railway Family' (*kokutetsu-ikka*), which signifies the Japanese National Railways. A union, incorporating both workers and management, calls this 'management–labour harmony'. Though it is often said that the traditional family (*ie*) institution has disappeared, the concept of the *ie* still persists in modern contexts. A company is conceived as an *ie*, all its employees qualifying as members of the household, with the employer at its head. Again this 'family' envelops the employee's personal family; it 'engages' him 'totally' (*marugakae* in Japanese). The employer readily takes responsibility for his employee's family, for which, in turn, the primary concern is the company, rather than relatives who reside elsewhere. (The features relating the company with its employees' families will be discussed later, pp. 14–15.) In this modern context, the employee's family, which normally comprises the employee himself, his wife and children, is a unit which can no longer be conceived as an *ie*, but simply a family. The unit is comparable to the family of a servant or clerk who worked in the master's *ie*, the managing body of the pre-modern enterprise. The role of the *ie* institution as the distinguished unit in society in pre-modern times is now played by the company. This social group consciousness symbolized in the concept of the *ie*, of being one unit within a frame, has been achievable at any time, has been promoted by slogans and justified in the traditional morality.

This analysis calls for a reconsideration of the stereotyped view that modernization or urbanization weakens kinship ties, and creates a new type of social organization on entirely different bases. Certainly industrialization produces a new type of organization, the formal structure of which may be closely akin to that found in modern western societies. However, this does not necessarily accord with changes in the informal structure, in which, as in the case of Japan, the traditional structure persists in large measure. This demonstrates that the basic social structure continues in spite of great changes in social organization.*

2 Emotional participation and one-to-one relationships

It is clear from the previous section that social groups constructed with particular reference to situation, i.e. frame, include members with differing attributes. A group formed on the basis of

---

* I think that, in this analysis, it is effective and convenient to employ the differentiated concepts, *social structure* and *social organization*, as proposed by Raymond Firth ('Social Organization and Social Change', *Journal of the Royal Anthropological Institute*, vol. 84, pp. 1–20, 1954; the same paper appears as Chapter III of *Essays on Social Organization and Values*, 1964).

commonality of attribute can possess a strong sense of exclusiveness, based on this homogeneity, even without recourse to any form of law. Naturally, the relative strength of this factor depends on a variety of conditional circumstances, but in the fundamentals of group formation this homogeneity among group members stands largely by its own strength, and conditions are secondary. When a group develops on the situational basis of frame the primary form is a simple herd which in itself does not possess internal positive elements which can constitute a social group. Constituent elements of the group in terms of their attributes may be heterogenous but may not be complementary. (The discussion here does not link to Durkheimian Theory as such; the distinction is between societies where people stick together because they are similar and those where they stick together because they are complementary.) For example, a group of houses built in the same area may form a village simply by virtue of physical demarcation from other houses. But in order to create a functional corporate group, there is need of an internal organization which will link these independent households. In such a situation some sort of law must be evolved to guide group coherence.

In addition to the initial requirement of a strong, enduring frame, there is need to strengthen the frame even further and to make the group element tougher. Theoretically, this can be done in two ways. One is to influence the members within the frame in such a way that they have a feeling of 'one-ness'; the second method is to create an internal organization which will tie the individuals in the group to each other and then to strengthen this organization. In practice, both these modes occur together, are bound together and progress together; they become, in fact, one common rule of action, but for the sake of convenience I shall discuss them separately. In this section I discuss the feeling of unity; in the following chapter I shall consider internal organization.

People with different attributes can be led to feel that they are members of the same group, and that this feeling is justified, by stressing the group consciousness of 'us' against 'them', i.e. the external, and by fostering a feeling of rivalry against other similar

9

groups. In this way there develops internally the sentimental tie of 'members of the same troop'.

Since disparity of attribute is a rational thing, an emotional approach is used to overcome it. This emotional approach is facilitated by continual human contact of the kind that can often intrude on those human relations which belong to the completely private and personal sphere. Consequently, the power and influence of the group not only affects and enters into the individual's actions; it alters even his ideas and ways of thinking. Individual autonomy is minimized. When this happens, the point where group or public life ends and where private life begins no longer can be distinguished. There are those who perceive this as a danger, an encroachment on their dignity as individuals; on the other hand, others feel safer in total-group consciousness. There seems little doubt that the latter group is in the majority. Their sphere of living is usually concentrated solely within the village community or the place of work. The Japanese regularly talk about their homes and love affairs with co-workers; marriage within the village community or place of work is prevalent; the family frequently participates in company pleasure trips. The provision of company housing, a regular practice among Japan's leading enterprises, is a good case in point. Such company houses are usually concentrated in a single area and form a distinct entity within, say, a suburb of a large city. In such circumstances employees' wives come into close contact with and are well informed about their husbands' activities. Thus, even in terms of physical arrangements, a company with its employees and their families forms a distinct social group. In an extreme case, a company may have a common grave for its employees, similar to the household grave. With group-consciousness so highly developed there is almost no social life outside the particular group on which an individual's major economic life depends. The individual's every problem must be solved within this frame. Thus group participation is simple and unitary. It follows then that each group or institution develops a high degree of independence and closeness, with its own internal law which is totally binding on members.

The archetype of this kind of group is the Japanese 'household' (*ie*) as we have described it in the previous section. In Japan, for example, the mother-in-law and daughter-in-law problem is preferably solved inside the household, and the luckless bride has to struggle through in isolation, without help from her own family, relatives or neighbours. By comparison, in agricultural villages in India not only can the bride make long visits to her parental home but her brother may frequently visit her and help out in various ways. Mother-in-law and daughter-in-law quarrels are conducted in raised voices that can be heard all over the neighbourhood, and when such shouting is heard all the women (of the same caste) in the neighbourhood come over to help out. The mutual assistance among the wives who come from other villages is a quite enviable factor completely unimaginable among Japanese women. Here again the function of the social factor of attribute (wife) is demonstrated; it supercedes the function of the frame of the household. In Japan, by contrast, 'the parents step in when their children quarrel' and, as I shall explain in detail later, the structure is the complete opposite to that in India.

Moral ideas such as 'the husband leads and the wife obeys' or 'man and wife are one flesh' embody the Japanese emphasis on integration. Among Indians, however, I have often observed husband and wife expressing quite contradictory opinions without the slightest hesitation. This is indeed rare in front of others in Japan. The traditional authority of the Japanese household head, once regarded as the prime characteristic of the family system, extended over the conduct, ideas and ways of thought of the household's members, and on this score the household head could be said to wield a far greater power than his Indian counterpart. In Indian family life there are all kinds of rules that apply in accordance with the status of the individual family member; the wife, for instance, must not speak directly to her husband's elder brothers, father, etc. These rules all relate to individual behaviour, but in the sphere of ideas and ways of thought the freedom and strong individuality permitted even among members of the same family is surprising to a Japanese. The rules, moreover, do not differ from household to household, but are common to the whole community, and especially among the members of the same caste community. In other words, the rules are of universal character, rather than being situational or particular to each household, as is the case in Japan.* Compared with traditional Japanese family life, the extent to which members of an Indian household are bound by the individual household's traditional practices is very small.

An Indian who had been studying in Japan for many years once compared Japanese and Indian practice in the following terms:

Why does a Japanese have to consult his companions over even the most trivial matter? The Japanese always call a conference about the slightest thing, and hold frequent meetings, though these are mostly informal, to decide everything. In India, we have definite rules as family members (and this is also true of other social groups), so that when one wants to do something one knows whether it is all right by instantaneous reflection on those rules – it is not necessary to consult with the head or with other members of the family. Outside these rules, you are largely free to act as an individual; whatever you do, you have only to ask whether or not it will run counter to the rules.

As this clearly shows, in India 'rules' are regarded as a definite but abstract social form, not as a concrete and individualized form particular to each family/social group as is the case in Japan. The individuality of the Indian family unit is not strong, nor is there group participation by family members of the order of the emotional participation in the Japanese household; nor is the family as a living unit (or as a group holding communal property) a closed community as in the case of the Japanese household. Again, in contrast to Japanese practice, the individual in India is strongly tied to the social network outside his household.

In contrast to the Japanese system, the Indian system allows freedom in respect of ideas and ways of thought as opposed to conduct. I believe for this reason, even though there are economic and ethical restrictions on the modernization of society, the Indian does not see his traditional family system as an enemy of progress

* Certainly there exists what may be called a standard norm or commonality which is shared by Japanese households as a whole (or, more precisely, by a local community or different strata), but within this context each individual household normally has its own ways to regulate the behaviour and speech of individual members.

to such a degree as the Japanese does. This view may contradict that conventionally held by many people on Indian family. It is important to note that the comparison here is made between Japanese and Hindu systems focused on actual interpersonal relationships within the family or household, rather than between western and Indian family patterns in a general outlook. I do not intend here to present the structure and workings of actual personal relations in Japanese and Hindu families in detail, but the following point would be some help to indicate my point. In the ideal traditional household in Japan, for example, opinions of the members of the household should always be held unanimously regardless of the issue, and this normally meant that all members accepted the opinion of the household head, without even discussing the issue. An expression of a contradictory opinion to that of the head was considered a sign of misbehaviour, disturbing the harmony of the group order. Contrasted to such a unilateral process of decision making in the Japanese household, the Indian counterpart allows much room for discussion between its members; they, whether sons, wife or even daughters, are able to express their views much more freely and they in fact can enjoy a discussion, although the final decision may be taken by the head. Hindu family structure is similar hierarchically to the Japanese family, but the individual's rights are well preserved in it. In the Japanese system all members of the household are in one group under the head, with no specific rights according to the status of individuals within the family. The Japanese family system differs from that of the Chinese system, where family ethics are always based on relationships between particular individuals such as father and son, brothers and sisters, parent and child, husband and wife, while in Japan they are always based on the collective group, i.e., members of a household, not on the relationships between individuals.

The Japanese system naturally produces much more frustration in the members of lower status in the hierarchy; and allows the head to abuse the group or an individual member. In Japan, especially immediately after the second world war, the idea has gained ground that the family system (*ie*) was an evil, feudalistic growth obstructing modernization, and on this premise one could point out the evil uses to which the unlimited infiltration of the household head's authority were put. It should be noticed here, however, that although the power of each individual household head is often regarded as exclusively his own, in fact it is the social group, the 'household', which has the ultimate integrating power, a power which restricts each member's behaviour and thought, including that of the household head himself.

Another group characteristic portrayed in the Japanese household can be seen when a business enterprise is viewed as a social group. In this instance a closed social group has been organized on the basis of the 'life-time employment system' and the work made central to the employees' lives. The new employee is in just about the same position and is, in fact, received by the company in much the same spirit as if he were a newly born family member, a newly adopted son-in-law or a bride come into the husband's household. A number of well-known features peculiar to the Japanese employment system illustrate this characteristic, for example, company housing, hospital benefits, family-recreation groups for employees, monetary gifts from the company on the occasion of marriage, birth or death and even advice from the company's consultant on family planning. What is interesting here is that this tendency is very obvious even in the most forward-looking, large enterprises or in supposedly modern, advanced management. The concept is even more evident in Japan's basic payment system, used by every industrial enterprise and government organization, in which the family allowance is the essential element. This is also echoed in the principle of the seniority payment system.

The relationship between employer and employee is not to be explained in contractual terms. The attitude of the employer is expressed by the spirit of the common saying, 'the enterprise is the people'. This affirms the belief that employer and employee are bound as one by fate in conditions which produce a tie between man and man often as firm and close as that between husband and wife. Such a relationship is manifestly not a purely contractual one between employer and employee; the employee is already a member of his own family, and all members of his family are naturally included in the larger company 'family'. Employers do not employ only a man's labour itself but really employ the total man, as is shown in the expression *marugakae* (completely enveloped). This trend can be traced consistently in Japanese management from the Meiji period to the present.

The life-time employment system, characterized by the integral and lasting commitment between employee and employer, contrasts sharply with the high mobility of the worker in the United States. It has been suggested that this system develops from Japan's economic situation and is closely related to the surplus of labour. However, as J.C.Abegglen has suggested in his penetrating analysis (*The Japanese Factory*, 1958, Chapter 2), the immobility of Japanese labour is not merely an economic problem. That it is also closely related to the nature of Japanese social structure will become evident from my discussion. In fact, Japanese labour relations in terms of surplus and shortage of labour have least affected the life-time employment system. In fact, these contradictory situations have together contributed to the development of the system.

It might be appropriate at this point to give a brief description of the history of the development of the life-time employment system in Japan. In the early days of Japan's industrialization, there was a fairly high rate of movement of factory workers from company to company, just as some specific type of workmen or artisans of pre-industrial urban Japan had moved freely from job to job. Such mobility in some workers in pre-industrial and early industrial Japan, seems to be attributed to the following reasons: a specific type of an occupation, the members of which consisted of a rather small percentage of the total working population and the demand for them was considerably high; these workers were located in a situation outside well established institutionalized systems. The mobility of factory workers caused uncertainty and inconvenience to employers in their efforts to retain a constant labour force. To counteract this fluidity, management policy gradually moved in the direction of keeping workers in the company for their entire working lives, rather than towards developing a system based on contractual arrangements. By the beginning of this century larger enterprises were already starting to develop management policies based on this principle; they took the form of various welfare benefits, company houses at nominal rent, commissary purchasing facilities and the like. This trend became particularly marked after the first world war when the shortage of labour was acute.

It was also at the end of the first world war that there came into practice among large companies the regular employment system by which a company takes on each spring a considerable number of boys who have just left school. This development arose from the demand for company-trained personnel adapted to the mechanized production systems that followed the introduction of new types of machinery from Germany and the United States. Boys fresh from school were the best potential labour force for mechanized industry because they were more easily moulded to suit a company's requirements. They were trained by the company not only technically but also morally. In Japan it has always been believed that individual moral and mental attitudes have an important bearing on productive power. Loyalty towards the company has been highly regarded. A man may be an excellent technician, but if his way of thought and his moral attitudes do not accord with the company's ideal the company does not hesitate to dismiss him. Men who move in from another company at a comparatively advanced stage in their working life tend to be considered difficult to mould or suspect in their loyalties. Ease of training, then, was the major reason why recruitment of workers was directed more and more towards boys fresh from school. (There is an excellent statement of conditions in Abegglen, *ibid.*, Chapter I.)

Recruitment methods thus paved the way for the development of the life-employment system. An additional device was evolved to hold workers to a company, for example, the seniority payment system based on duration of service, age and educational qualifications, with the added lure of a handsome payment on retirement. The principle behind this seniority system had the advantage of being closely akin to the traditional pattern of commercial and agricultural management in pre-industrial Japan. In these old-

be addressed as Tanaka-*san*, Tanaka-*kun* or Tanaka (i.e. without suffix). *San* is used for *sempai*, *kun* for *kōhai* and the name without suffix is reserved for *doryō*.* The last form is comparable with the English usage of addressing by the Christian name.† But the use of this form is carefully restricted to those who are very close to oneself. Even among *dōryō*, *san* is used towards those with whom one is not sufficiently familiar, while *kun* is used between those closer than those addressed by *san*, former class-mates, for example. A relationship which permits of address by surname only is of a specifically familiar nature, not unlike the French usage of *tu*. Therefore, a man may also address very intimate *kōhai* in this way, but these *kōhai* will use the *san* form of address to him. In the case of professionals, within this pattern, a *sempai* is addressed as *sensei* instead of *san*, *sensei* being the higher honorific term, used of teachers by their students, and also of professionals by the general public.

It is important to note that this usage of terms of address, once determined by relationships in the earlier stages of a man's life or career, remains unchanged for the rest of his life. Let us imagine, for example, the case of X, once a student of Y, who, fifteen years afterwards, becomes a professor in the same department as Y and thus acquires equal status. X still addresses Y as *sensei* and will not refer to him as *dōryō* (colleague) to a third person. Y may address X as *kun*, treating him, that is, as *kōhai*, even in front of X's students or outsiders: Y has to be most broad-minded and sociable to address X as *sensei* in such a context (i.e. the English usage of Dr or Professor).

It may also be that when X is well known, but Y is not, Y may intentionally address X as *kun* in public in order to indicate that, 'he is superior to X, X is only his *kōhai*'. It is the general tendency to indicate one's relatively higher status; this practice derives from

---

* *San* is the most general form of address, equivalent to Mr, Mrs or Miss. The differentiations here discussed apply only to men: women do not use such elaborate address terms in general social life, though in a special group (for example, among *geisha*) a similar pattern is found in the usage of different terms.

† The use of the first name in Japan is confined mainly to children. Among adults, it is employed only in relation to those who had close relations in childhood. One is addressed by the first name only by parents, siblings, close relatives and childhood friends.

the fact that the ranking order is perceived as ego-centred. Once established, vertical ranking functions as the charter of the social order, so that whatever the change in an individual's status, popularity or fame, there is a deeply ingrained reluctance to ignore or change the established order.

The relative rankings are thus centred on ego and everyone is placed in a relative locus within the firmly established vertical system. Such a system works against the formation of distinct strata within a group, which, even if it consists of homogeneous members in terms of qualification, tends to be organized according to hierarchical order. In this kind of society ranking becomes far more important than any differences in the nature of the work, or of status group. Even among those with the same training, qualifications or status, differences based on rank are always perceptible, and because the individuals concerned are deeply aware of the existence of such distinctions, these tend to overshadow and obscure even differences of occupation, status or class.

The precedence of elder over younger (chō-yō-no-jo) reflects the well-known moral ethic which was imported from China at a comparatively early stage in Japan's history. However, the Japanese application of this concept in actual life seems to have been somewhat different from that of the Chinese. An interesting example illustrates this discrepancy. When six Chinese shōgi (chess) players came to Japan recently to play against the Japanese, one thing that struck Japanese observers was the ranking order of the six players. In the account of their arrival carried by Asahi-shimbun, one of the leading Japanese daily newspapers, it was reported that Mr Wan, aged 17, the youngest of the six, stood fourth in order at the welcoming ceremony at Haneda Airport, and again at the reception party in Tokyo. The reporter went on to observe,

If we regard them according to the Japanese way of according precedence, Mr Wan, who is the youngest of them all and holds only nidan (second rank), should occupy the last seat in place of Mr Tsen, who though the eldest in years now takes the lowest place. They, however, take as the basis for position the order which resulted from the last title-match standings.

28

The Chinese are not always as conscious of order (seniority and rank, that is) as are the Japanese; they limit the effectiveness of seniority or rank to certain activities or situations and eliminate it from others. From what I have been able to observe, although the Chinese always appreciate manners which show respect towards those in a senior position, senior and junior might well stand on an equal footing in certain circumstances. The Chinese are able to readjust the order, or work according to a ranking established by a different criterion, by merit, for example, if the latter suits the circumstances.

In Japan once rank is established on the basis of seniority, it is applied to all circumstances, and to a great extent controls social life and individual activity. Seniority and merit are the principal criteria for the establishment of a social order; every society employs these criteria, although the weight given to each may differ according to social circumstances. In the west merit is given considerable importance, while in Japan the balance goes the other way. In other words, in Japan, in contrast to other societies, the provisions for recognition of merit are weak, and institutionalization of the social order has been effected largely by means of seniority; this is the more obvious criterion, assuming an equal ability in individuals entering the same kind of service.

The system of ranking by seniority is a simpler and more stable mechanism than the merit system, since, once it is set, it works automatically without need of any form of regulation or check. But at the same time this system brings with it a high degree of rigidity. There is only one ranking order for a given set of persons, regardless of variety of situation. No individual member of this set (not even the man who ranks highest) can make even a partial change. The only means of effecting change is by some drastic event which affects the principle of the order, or by the disintegration of the group.

It is because of this rigidity and stability that are produced by ranking that the latter functions as the principal controlling factor of social relations in Japan. The basic orientation of the social order permeates every aspect of society, far beyond the limits of the institutionalized group. This ranking order, in effect, regulates Japanese life.

In everyday affairs a man who has no awareness of relative rank is not able to speak or even sit and eat. When speaking, he is expected always to be ready with differentiated, delicate degrees of honorific expressions appropriate to the rank order between himself and the person he addresses. The expressions and the manner appropriate to a superior are never to be used to an inferior. Even among colleagues, it is only possible to dispense with honorifics when both parties are very intimate friends. In such contexts the English language is inadequate to supply appropriate equivalents. Behaviour and language are intimately interwoven in Japan.

The ranking order within a given institution affects not only the members of that institution but through them it affects the establishment of relations between persons from different institutions when they meet for the first time. On such occasions the first thing that the Japanese do is exchange name cards. This act has crucial social implications. Not only do name cards give information about the name (and the characters with which it is written) and the address; their more important function is to make clear the title, the position and the institution of the person who dispenses them. It is considered proper etiquette for a man to read carefully what is printed on the card, and to adjust his behaviour, mode of address and so on in accordance with the information it gives him. By exchanging cards, both parties can gauge the relationship between them in terms of relative rank, locating each other within the known order of their society.* Only after this is done are they able to speak with assurance, since, before they can do so, they must be sure of the degree of honorific content and politeness they must put into their words.

In the west there are also certain codes which differentiate appropriate behaviour according to the nature of the relation between the speaker and the second person. But in Japan the range of differentiation is much wider and more elaborate, and delicate codification is necessary to meet each context and situation. I was asked one day by a French journalist who had just arrived in

* See Chapter 3, particularly pp. 92-3 for detailed explanation.

Tokyo to explain why a man changes his manner, depending upon the person he is addressing, to such a degree that the listener can hardly believe him to be the same speaker. This Frenchman had observed that even the voice changes (which could well be true, since he had no knowledge of Japanese and so was unable to notice the use of differentiating honorific words; he sensed the difference only from variations in sound).

Certainly there are personal differences in the degree to which people observe the rules of propriety, and there are also differences related to the varying situations in which they are involved, with the result that the examples I have quoted may be felt to be rather extreme. Some flaunt their higher status by haughtiness towards inferiors and excessive modesty towards superiors; others may prefer to conceal haughtiness, remaining modest even towards inferiors, a manner which is appreciated by the latter and may result in greater benefit to the superior. And some are simply less conscious of the order of rank, although these would probably account for only a rather small percentage.

But whatever the variations in individual behaviour, awareness of rank is deeply rooted in Japanese social behaviour. In describing an individual's personality, a Japanese will normally derive his objective criteria from a number of social patterns currently established. Institutional position and title constitute one of the major criteria, while a man's individual qualities tend to be overlooked.

Without consciousness of ranking, life could not be carried on smoothly in Japan, for rank is the social norm on which Japanese life is based. In a traditional Japanese house the arrangement of a room manifests this gradation of rank and clearly prescribes the ranking differences which are to be observed by those who use it. The highest seat is always at the centre backed by the *tokonoma* (alcove), where a painted scroll is hung and flowers are arranged; the lowest seat is nearest the entrance to the room. This arrangement never allows two or more individuals to be placed as equals. Whatever the nature of the gathering, those present will eventually establish a satisfactory order among themselves, after each of them has shown the necessary preliminaries of the etiquette of self-effacement. Status, age, popularity, sex, etc., are elements which contribute to the fixing of the order, but status is without exception the dominant factor.* A guest is always placed higher than the host unless his status is much lower than that of the host. A guest coming from a more distant place is accorded particularly respectful treatment.

There is no situation as awkward in Japan as when the appropriate order is ignored or broken – when, for example, an inferior sits at a seat higher than that of his superior. It is often agreed that, in these 'modern' days, the younger generation tends to infringe the rules of order. But it is interesting to note that young people soon begin to follow the traditional order once they are employed, as they gradually realize the social cost that such infringement involves. The young Japanese, moreover, is never free of the seniority system. In schools there is a very distinct senior–junior ranking among students, which is observed particularly strictly among those who form sports clubs. In a student mountaineering club, for example, it is the students of a junior class who carry a heavier load while climbing, pitch the tent and prepare the evening meal under the surveillance of the senior students, who may sit smoking. When the preparations are over it is the senior students who take the meal first, served by the junior students. This strong rank consciousness, it is said, clearly reflects the practices of the former Japanese army.

In the west the use of a regulated table plan is restricted usually to occasions such as a formal dinner party, when the chief guest is placed at the right of the host and so on. But in Japan even at the supper table of a humble family there is no escape from the formality demanded by rank. At the start of the meal everyone

---

* Age and sex are superseded by status. For example, the head of a household, regardless of age, occupies the highest seat; his retired father retreats to a lower seat. Age will become a deciding factor only among persons of similar status. Status also precedes sex. It is well known that Japanese women are nearly always ranked as inferiors; this is not because their sex is considered inferior, but because women seldom hold higher social status. Difference of sex will never be so pronounced in Japanese thinking as in America, where classification (though not for purposes of establishing rank) is primarily by sex. I am convinced that in American society sex-consciousness predominates over status-consciousness, the exact opposite of Japan.

should be served cooked rice by the mistress of the household. The bowls should be served in order of rank, from higher to lower: among family members, for example, the head of the household will be served first, followed by his nominal successor (his son or adopted son-in-law), other sons and daughters according to sex and seniority. Last of all come the mistress of the household and the wife of the successor. The sequence of serving thus clearly reflects the structure of the group.

Since ranking order appears so regularly in such essential aspects of daily life, the Japanese cannot help but be made extremely conscious of it. In fact, this consciousness is so strong that official rank is easily extended into private life. A superior in one's place of work is always one's superior wherever he is met, at a restaurant, at home, in the street. When wives meet, they, too, will behave towards each other in accordance with the ranks of their husbands, using honorific expressions and gestures appropriate to the established relationship between their husbands. A leader in Japan tends to display his leadership in any and every circumstance, even when leadership is in no way called for. American behaviour is quite different in this particular: my experience among Americans is that it is often very difficult to discover even who is the leader of a group (or who has higher or lower status), except in circumstances which require that the leadership make itself known.

A fixed seating order, particularly appropriate to and impressive in a Japanese-style room, extends also to the modern western-style room. At any gathering or meeting it is obvious at first glance which is the most superior and the most inferior person present. The frequency with which a man offers an opinion, together with the order in which those present speak at the beginning of the meeting, are further indications of rank. A man who sits near the entrance may speak scarcely at all throughout the meeting. In a very delicate situation those of an inferior status would not dare to laugh earlier or louder than their superiors, and most certainly would never offer opinions contradictory to those of their superiors. To this extent, ranking order not only regulates social behaviour but also curbs the open expression of thought.

In such manners we can observe how deep the ranking consciousness operates among Japanese. In this regard, I recall Tibetans, the pattern of whose everyday manners is very similar to that of the Japanese, in that they employ gestures and varying degrees of linguistic honorifics according to the difference in recognized ranks between speakers. However, I observed that when Tibetan scholars sit for a debate they completely renounce all difference of rank and stand equal to each other. I was told that even the Dalai Lama is no exception to this practice. Japanese scholars, on the other hand, never escape from the consciousness of the distinction between *sempai* and *kōhai*, even in the case of purely academic debates. It is very difficult for a Japanese scholar to disagree openly with a statement of his *sempai*. Even a trifling opposition to or disagreement with the *sempai*'s views involves an elaborate and roundabout drill. First, the objector should introduce a long appraisal of the part of the *sempai*'s work in question, using extremely honorific terms, and then gradually present his own opinion or opposition in a style which will give the impression that his opposition is insignificant, being afraid to hurt his *sempai*'s feelings. The ranking of *sempai* and *kōhai* thus stifles the free expression of individual thought.*

The consciousness of rank which leads the Japanese to ignore logical procedure is also manifested in the patterns and practices of daily conversation, in which a senior or an elderly man monopolizes the talk while those junior to them have the role of listener. Generally there is no development of dialectic style in a Japanese conversation, which is guided from beginning to end by the interpersonal relations which exist between the speakers. In most cases a conversation is either a one-sided sermon, the 'I agree completely' style of communication, which does not allow for the statement of opposite views; or parties to a conversation follow parallel lines, winding in circles and ending exactly where they started. Much of a conversation is taken up by long descriptive accounts, the narration of personal experiences or the statement of an attitude towards a person or an event in definitive and

---

* The ranking of *sempai* and *kōhai* is determined by the year of graduation from university, which is always one of the narrow group of leading universities.

The formation of groups occurs not only at the occupational level but also at various minor levels; again, smaller groups may be formed within a minor group. Among scholars, specialists in a particular field may be formed into groups divided according to school loyalties; these may be augmented into smaller sub-groups which come together on the basis of more intimate relations. It is this smallest group that has the significant function; its core may consist of several scholars who share a common view and style of approach, derived from a single ruling theory. A group normally has its central figure to whom the other members attach, often emotionally, on the basis of former professor–student or class-mate relationships. A grouping of this nature, as with politicians, serves as a protection of the weaker, who might be forgotten or unproductive if forced back solely on their own resources. But this group structure has drawbacks in the development of science, for instance; group members meet very frequently, but rarely do they discuss issues with persons outside their group. In the course of time each group devises and promulgates its own peculiar styles of expression and parochial terms, not understandable to the outsider even though he works in the same field of specialization. Such obstacles to productive discussion make it difficult for scholar-groups in Japan even to reach mutual understanding.

If, even among themselves, Japanese specialists have difficulties in communication, in the domain of international affairs they find their problems compounded. One of the best-known political scientists, who leads a large group of disciples, confessed recently on his return from Europe and America that foreigners' problems are so different from *ours* that he could not easily communicate with them. (It is my contention that he can speak only for himself and his group, not for Japanese specialists as a whole. However, this is indeed a difficulty for many Japanese scholars, and particularly for those who specialize in the social sciences.)

Curricula and standards of teaching in Japanese higher education are not very different from those of western countries. The difficulty facing scholars arises from the insularity which they themselves have occasioned, for Japan as a nation experiences this same localism because of the handicap of the lack of direct than nepotism in other societies. And when an individual's place in his group is governed solely by the length of his actual contact with the group, contact itself becomes the individual's private social capital. Because this capital is not transferable to any other group, the individual cannot shift from one group to another without undergoing very great social loss. Even if a man's company abandoned the seniority system and he could move to a new job at the same or a higher salary, so that a move entailed no actual economic loss, the social loss would remain (see pp. 105-106).

In conjunction with the factor of the absolute time span, an additional factor of temporary loss of tangibility may enter into the operation of the direct contact element. A group member who is absent temporarily may well lose ground within the group, for a period of separation often alienates existing contacts. When a man working in Tokyo leaves for another post elsewhere his departure implies not only a physical separation from the city itself but also the growth of social distance from his circle. 'The person who leaves gets more distant day by day' sums it all up; hence the strong sense of tragedy that the Japanese feel in farewells.

There is no alienation, loneliness or irritability comparable to that of the Japanese whose work takes him to a foreign country. 'They've probably completely forgotten me', and 'That colleague of mine back home has probably played his cards so well that he'll be a manager in no time' – such apprehensions suggest the wretched atmosphere built round himself by the Japanese exile. To diminish the sense of separation a little, he writes letters diligently. But to those he left back in Japan he 'gets more distant day by day', so the replies gradually get fewer and further between, and finally non-business connections cease entirely. He becomes weary of waiting for the order to return home and when at last the long-awaited permission is granted and he returns to his old job it somehow just is not the same. It is clearly a social 'minus' to have been away. He will have to spend an uncomfortable period until he again becomes accustomed and readjusted to his old group, the climate of which may well have changed since he left. In fact, it often happens that the promotion of a man who has stayed abroad for a certain period of time is delayed longer than those of his colleagues (*dōryō*) who have served continuously in the main office. This does not necessarily apply, of course, in the case of a company where business requires able men to reside abroad; in this case the various branch offices abroad are ranked on the regular promotion ladder. Even so, however, the man posted abroad finds it hard not to feel out of the mainstream of developments in his firm's affairs. Most of Japanese men abroad are quite homesick, and very concerned with personnel affairs in the home office. It is not surprising, then, that the Japanese does not like to leave his own community for very long periods; he is very prone to the apprehension that too long a period of absence will lead automatically to an inability to keep up-to-date and to retain standards. This means being excluded from the activities of his old group.

In contrast with the Japanese ideal of group participation, a group formed on the basis of attribute maintains ties with a member no matter where he lives or works, because of its network, which can overcome separation in terms of both space and time. Thus an Indian or Chinese living abroad can get on with his work calmly and live comfortably because of the existence of this network. Further, an Indian born in Africa or elsewhere abroad could go back to live in his grandfather's village and his presence would be taken for granted. He would be received easily by the villagers, even though they did not know his face, or even his father's or grandfather's. They would accept him because he is linked to the village by patrilineal kinship.

But a Japanese in similar circumstances would have to face a very uncomfortable situation and would not be likely to summon the courage to go back to live in his grandfather's village. The villagers would say, 'That is a new face that we don't know'; they would say to him, 'Nobody remembers your grandfather; people of his generation are all dead. Things have changed a lot here.' He would be treated as an outsider and, even if he were finally accepted, he would probably be placed at the bottom of the hierarchy, without being given the full rights of village membership. He would be expected to make a handsome donation to the communal fund, in the same way as would be expected of any unrelated newcomer. In daily life he would be left alone and would remain outside the social life of the community; because his habits and interests are quite different from those of the villagers, it would be difficult to arrive at any form of mutual understanding. Here, the invisible kinship link is not adequate to establish the legitimacy of the relation between him and the villagers. But in a Hindu community legitimacy of kinship survives against the ruptures of time and space to preserve the personal relation.

A Japanese who has been away from his home village for a long period is reluctant to go back, even though he usually has a sentimental attachment to it. He will say, 'My parents are already dead, my brothers and sisters are very old, it's now the turn of my nephews. You can't expect anything from them.' Or, 'It's a new generation since I went away. I don't know them well.' Kinship linkage may, however, have rather more efficacy in the reverse case, when a cousin, nephew or niece from the home village asks for the help of the ex-villager on moving to the city where the latter lives.

Ties of kinship, friendship or group membership all tend to diminish through physical separation. Even a reduction in the frequency of meetings with a friend causes one's rights and voice in the relationship to decrease accordingly. It has long been true that a Japanese who knows the Chinese and the English well has been deeply impressed by and has even envied the constancy and steadiness of their personal relationships in spite of long periods of separation. Tangibility in a personal relationship is a vital element in the creation of unity, particularly in a group which has no universal rules, but there is little equipment to resist breaches made by time and space. Even for a person physically present in the group, an emotional clash could entail the loss of a friendship. Tangibility is a very unstable support for the group. But at the same time it does facilitate the achievement of a condition in which recruitment is always open at the bottom of the hierarchy and in which anyone can be a candidate. Though it contributes to instability, it also offers the opportunity to adjust in the face of changing circumstances.

To summarize: while a Japanese attaches great importance to

concreteness and appreciates readiness to react to a changing situation, he does not trust nor establish a universal law, the nature of which is to be divorced from immediate actuality, although adaptable to any circumstance. Japan has no native concept of 'organization' or 'network' abstracted or divorced from actual man; 'organization' is perceived as a kind of succession of direct and concrete relationships between man and man. Man's concrete existence itself forms a part of 'organization'. This is to be seen very clearly, for example, in the development of residential areas in the suburbs of a large city. Private houses are built sporadically, in-filling follows and when, in the course of time, there grow clusters of houses residents realize the need for roads and, finally, narrow roads will be built, winding in such a way as to serve every house in the cluster. Such irregularity is not confined to the roads but is to be found also in the numbering of the houses, which goes by the order in which they were built rather than by the geographical order of the blocks or the location of the house unit. As a result, house numbering is in no way logical, and the stranger cannot possibly find a house simply by its number.

It is indeed surprising that little effort is made – by either planners or residents – to build roads or lay down plans for blocks or areas before work begins on the houses. The vast residential areas of Tokyo are the most telling example of the Japanese concept of 'organization'; these areas spread, literally, like amoeba! Surprisingly enough, processes such as these have improved hardly at all during the last hundred years, in contrast with the startling developments in industry. Certainly one can find the occasional well-planned residential area built by one of the large estate companies, but this is the exception; the more regular circumstances indicate the strength of the indigenous sociological forces in the face of great technical improvements. Techniques can easily be imported and improved, but it is very difficult to change the inherent system of social organization.

Tangibility, the essential element in 'organization' for the Japanese, may well have some bearing also on Japanese religious concepts. Japanese culture has no conception of a God existing abstractly, completely separate from the human world. In the ultimate analysis, the Japanese consciousness of the object of religious devotion grows out of direct-contact relations between individuals; it is conceived as an extension of this mediating tie. What is termed ancestor worship in Japan is quite different from that of the Chinese: it visualizes and is based on a concrete conception of ancestors in a series of generations going back directly from the dead parent to the founder of the house in which the family is domiciled. The recognized lineage of ancestors is fairly short, hardly going back further than those forefathers who live in the memory as quite concrete personal figures. Even the Emperor, with his ancestors, is conceptualized as the ultimate figure of successive lineal extensions of such actual links common to all Japanese through their respective ancestors: he is not a sacred figure divorced from his people.

CONCLUDING REMARKS

The analysis presented in the previous chapters of various Japanese group organizations reveals the vertical structural principle, the core of which is to be found in the basic social relationship between two individuals. This structural tendency, developing in the course of the history of the Japanese people, has become one of the characteristics of Japanese culture.

Certain factors have encouraged this tendency. The first is the homogeneous configuration of Japanese society. Archaeological research has shown that during the Jōmon period a single culture spread over the whole of Japan: between this time and the beginning of the historical period (fifth century AD), continental culture along with wet paddy cultivation may have left a considerable influence, particularly in western Japan, and may have helped the development of the Japanese state formation, but the numbers of continentals actually moving into Japan seems to be very small, and these were quickly and readily absorbed into the native population, so that there is no indication that these new elements formed a separate stratum from the Japanese. There is no evidence of significant movement into the islands of non-Japanese after this period.

Local powers and cultures developed during the medieval period, but these were no more than variations of the native pattern. During the Tokugawa period the centralized feudal system under the Shogunate assisted the development of an institutional homogeneity on top of the basic cultural homogeneity. In Tokugawa Japan peasants formed more than 80 per cent of the population, the *bushi* – the top status group – accounted for a further 6 per cent

It is used particularly as a charge against the monopoly of power by a privileged sector or a stronger faction in an organization. It is interesting to observe, however, that the form in which this charge is stated is identical with that through which authoritarian power has been exercised. The change from 'feudalism' to 'democracy' is not structural or organizational; it is rather a change in the direction of the motion of energy within the same pipeline, this energy exerted by the same kinds of people.

What the Japanese mean by 'democracy' is a system that should take the side of, or give consideration to, the weaker or lower; in practice, any decision should be made on the basis of a consensus which includes those located lower in the hierarchy. Such a consensus – reached by what might be termed maximum consultation – might seem a by-product of the post-war 'democratic' age; yet it is not at all new to the Japanese, representing as it does, a very basic style of the traditional group operation. The exercise of power or unilateral decision-making on the part of the top sector of a group co-existed with unanimous decision-making on the basis of maximum consultation. The difference between these two procedures, as I see it, derives from differences in the internal composition of a group (such as scale or manner) not in kinds of groups – such as differences in occupation, between rural and urban or younger and older.

The small group, of a dozen or less, with no significant status or economic differentiation between members, is most likely to function 'democratically' in the Japanese sense. Good examples of such a group can be found among many old-established villages, where the tradition has been to base any decision on maximum consultation. In addition to regular meetings, emergency gatherings are held whenever an urgent or major issue faces the village. To such a meeting every household sends a representative, normally the household head; in his absence, his wife or grown son deputizes. Such a meeting consists, ideally, of about ten persons. A village is always organized by sub-groups (local corporate groups) consisting of about ten households, and it is in these important functional groups that primary meetings are frequently held.

This is the size of gathering which the Japanese find most

satisfactory and enjoyable. It is usual in such a gathering for every participant, whether he be poor and lower in rank or not, to express an opinion. Relaxed and informal talk at the start induces a free atmosphere, as a kind of warm-up for the meeting proper. It is most important that a meeting should reach a unanimous conclusion; it should leave no one frustrated or dissatisfied, for this weakens village or group unity and solidarity. The undercurrent of feeling is: 'After all we are in the same boat, and we should live peacefully without leaving anyone behind as a straggler.' In order to reach unanimity, they do not care how long it takes – whatever time and trouble they may have in its procedure, all should reach a final consensus.

The process of discussion is not necessarily logical. They talk about this and that, often with much indulgence towards the individual feelings at stake. A meeting may take a recess when it comes to a deadlock, and will be resumed later in a fresh mood. In the course of time dissension decreases, and consent increases. When it reaches a stage where support comes from about 70 per cent of the members it is a sign of almost reaching a consensus. In the final stage the minority makes a concession, saying that 'I will join, since all of you have agreed. Though I dissent in this particular issue, by all means I am ready to co-operate with you, and at any rate I have been able to say all that I wanted to say.'

However, the procedure of a meeting of a large group does not allow sufficient time and, of course, the degree of differentiation in status and interest is much greater: as a result, members know less of each other, and many of them are reluctant to speak out. Such factors help to make the procedure of decision-making in these circumstances 'undemocratic'; the process is influenced by top members or a dominant clique and governed by the principle of majority rule, with scope for the effective use of hierarchical power relationships.

The urge towards maximum consultation, regardless of the nature and size of a group, frequently results in interminably long meetings, dragged out in the name of 'democracy'. Japan is today the land of meetings, and it is far from difficult to find a man who spends more time at meetings than at his desk. In group operation on the Japanese system there are few established rules and rôles are not clearly defined or distinguished, so that not only vital issues but those less pertinent are brought under consideration by a meeting. 'Democratic' procedure does not, of course, contribute to efficient modern management; but those at the top can make it a convenient excuse for a show of 'democracy', while, in fact, the decision is made by a 'boss' or influential members of the group, in disregard even of the function of the chairman. 'Democracy' may be in popular demand, but the old hierarchical structure functions latently under the façade and format of 'democracy'.

Apart from the so-called democratic procedure, I must also state how the Japanese man sees his organization. A Japanese cannot tolerate open discrimination by groups, or strata. As an illustration of this kind of feeling, I give here the following story of a *sararyman* (a Japanese term akin to 'organization man'). This person had an invitation from one of the western firms in Japan, looking for well-qualified Japanese staff. He was quite interested in the offer, which was far better than his job in a Japanese firm. However, he declined the offer because he had been informed by a friend employed in a western firm that in them only executives (westerners) used to enjoy coffee-breaks, while the Japanese subordinate staffs stayed at work. He felt a great humiliation and discrimination in it. Although in Japanese firms, top executives are often absent from their desks to attend weddings, funeral ceremonies or to play golf, he accepts these as the social duties of top men, and he also thinks that Japanese bosses sometimes share coffee or drink with him. On the other hand, he cannot accept seeing the bosses in the organization having a coffee-break while their subordinates are at work, and these western bosses never join him in coffee or for a drink.

Privileges of top men in Japanese groups can be seen in various ways – perhaps more obviously in their behaviour towards their subordinates – but their manners are not so clear-cut as executives versus line-officers, or clerks. Japanese men can tolerate the vertical power relationship between one-to-one, directly linked to each other, but they cannot do so in the form of a class or group. Here we see the mentality directly linked to that of peasants in olden days, who never used to see their masters or landlords forming an obvious status group, clearly separated from them. In their social world, on the contrary, a functional group was formed by landlords and tenants, master and servants. Their master or superior is always with them in a same group. The Japanese personal relationship between superior and subordinate may give an impression of unfairness on formal occasions – a subordinate usually being a 'yes-man', with much bowing to his boss, but it has a counterbalance through informal contacts which give the subordinate men a feeling of being 'in the same boat', or the same household. Japanese bosses consciously or unconsciously show to their subordinates on occasion a kind of behaviour in which the power relation of the formal organization is reversed. The philosophy of a Japanese man is that when you are in the same boat everybody should enjoy communal rights, regardless of differences in status and contributions. There is strong opposition to the formation of status groups within a single community, although the order of higher and lower in relationships between individuals is readily accepted.

It seems from these and similar considerations that Japanese 'democracy' is a kind of communitarian sentiment, with, as a major premise, a high degree of cohesion and consensus within the group. Liberalism with respect to opinion is not part of the concept, for 'democracy' may well be interpreted in terms of freedom of speech, by which is meant the freedom of the lower or the underprivileged to speak out; there is, however, no wish for opposition or realization of the function of opposition. In Japan it is extremely difficult to engage in a truly democratic discussion (of the type that I know from experience is common in India or, for instance, in Italy, England or America), in the course of which the statements of opposition are taken by the other party and then form an important element in the development of the discussion.

The Japanese interpretation of 'democracy', added to the characteristics and the value orientation already discussed, contributes to the strengthening of the solidarity of a group built of members of different qualification and status. The egalitarianism in the workings of a group, as has been noticed earlier (see p. 36), stands in the way of the formulation and the development of the concept of specialization and the incorporation of similar groups. We might well here recall the earlier discussion, in which was proposed the theory that the absence of division of labour assisted the development of the vertical system. Also important in this analysis is the absence of any type of organizational principle based on kinship networks as well as any sharp distinction between kin and non-kin. Since kinship factors cannot be used as an effective and primary charter of group organization, the bases are the locality and constant and tangible personal relations. I have already presented my analysis of the traditional rural community;* we now find the same principle in operation in modern communities.

The changes in Japanese society in the course of modernization have attracted much research and discussion. It has often been argued that the war brought a fundamental change in the Japanese; it might be truer to argue that since the circumstances and supports of life in Japan have altered radically, ideas and attitudes to life have in turn changed, just as clothes are changed with the coming spring after the cold winter. It is Japanese nature to accept change with little resistance and, indeed, to welcome and value change; but a superficial change of outlook, as facile as changes in fashion, has not the slightest effect on the firm persistence of the basic nature and core of personal relations and group dynamics.

Historians, sociologists, economists and social critics are concerned to follow processes of change. These may find fault with the analysis presented here as may well those cultural anthropologists who are not accustomed to structural analysis, on the charge that I disregard the changing aspects of Japanese society. In answer I should restate the aim of this study – not to describe Japanese society but to view Japanese social structure in the light of a cross-cultural comparison of social structures; this is the concern of social anthropology which distinguishes it from the other social sciences. I do not for the moment deny the changing aspects of Japanese society; but I believe that it is also most important to look for the persistent factors underlying the various changes. In a scientific cross-cultural comparison the constants

* See Nakane, *op.cit.*

148

are dealt with more effectively; aspects of change are more attractive for the description of the picture of Japan alone.

It is in informal systems rather than in overt cultural elements that persistent factors are to be found. The informal system, the driving force of Japanese activities, is a native Japanese brew, steeped in a unique characteristic of Japanese culture. In the course of modernization Japan imported many western cultural elements, but these were and are always partial and segmentary and are never in the form of an operating system. It is like a language with its basic indigenous structure or grammar which has accumulated a heavy overlay of borrowed vocabulary; while the outlook of Japanese society has suffered drastic changes over the past hundred years, the basic social grammar has hardly been affected. Here is an example of industrialization and the importation of western culture not effecting changes in the basic cultural structure.

This structural persistence manifests one of the distinctive characteristics of a homogeneous society built on a vertical organizational principle. Such a society is fairly stable; it is difficult to create revolution or disorder on a national scale, since there is segmentation of the lower sectors into various group clusters fenced off from each other. Structural difficulties stand in the way of a broad scope of joint activity – members of a trade union, for example, are too loyal to their own company to join forces with their brothers in other company unions; student unions are unable to muster the great majority of students, but develop groups where the solidarity of one group differentiates it from another. A union movement, a confrontation, whether it may be between the manager and workers or between the faculty and students, is always carried on within an institution, although it causes echoes generally and politically. It is like a domestic discord, so that it tends to be very emotional and radical. In an extreme case it may drive some of the directors or section heads to commit suicide. Within the last six months in the height of student revolts, three directors committed suicide; and very similar phenomena occurred during the earlier union movements in industrial fields soon after the war. These movements are felt most intensely by all those concerned, but they are always in contrast to the peaceful order of the social life of the general public which surrounds them. Thus trade or student unions and other popular movements, in spite of the strong appeal of radicalism and violence, have little social significance, in that they are unable to stir the majority, even of those in the same category.

Thus there is a cruelly heavy handicap against the powerless and the socially inferior. Indeed, there is no possibility of creating any kind of revolution. A rebellion against the bosses and appeals to the general public may result in some changes in public opinion, but will never succeed in changing the social structure. At the same time, although those at the top can as a group exercise power and influence to check these movements, an individual, however able, however strong his personality and high his status, has to compromise with his group's decision, which then develops a life of its own. Once a collective decision of this kind has been formulated, no individual can check or turn it, and must simply wait for the time when the tide turns by itself, just like peasants cultivating wet paddy, who long for good weather after the typhoon.

However, the basis which allows the formulation of such overriding group decisions seems to be in the inherent mentality of the people. The greatest concern for Japanese people takes always in a form of *relativism*. For example, their constant desire is to rise a little higher than the average: to put it in a Japanese way, 'a desire to be similar to the other fellows who are supposed to be higher than oneself'. The Japanese are devoid of any such religious practice as controls individual thinking and behaviour on the strength of a supernatural being. What plays an important rôle for the Japanese is not religion or philosophy but a very human morality. And this morality always governs people with the contemporary trends as a yardstick. A feeling that 'I must do this because they are also doing it' or 'because they will laugh at me unless I do so' rules the life of individual persons with greater force than anything else and thus affects decision-making. Certainly, there are those who keep an attitude of 'going-my-way', but they are exceptionally rare in Japanese society. It is said that younger people are becoming critical to this general attitude, and in fact such a tendency may weaken its force in the course of time. Nevertheless, this kind of social habit deeply rooted in Japanese society seems to continue as a dominant tendency. It is based on largely this kind of attitude that the Japanese people's ideals are liable to change more easily with the shift of the times when compared with the people of other societies. This also explains why the Japanese are often described as lacking in consistency or as having a high degree of adaptability.

It is on these grounds that the majority rule is always employed as a powerful device by a dominant group or sector of a group; and the power at the top, which is always formed by a dominant group, never as an individual, has always succeeded in imposing its aims, with even the law powerless to check them. It is obvious that political traits rather than social ones are decisive in a society of this kind. Throughout Japan's history, political activities have been more important than any others. This is the clue to Japan's efficiency – but it is also a source of danger, to Japanese society as a whole and to all the groups which constitute it. From this angle, Japan's record in the war (including the process towards the war) as well as the speed and force of her industrialization are also to be viewed.

INDEX

academics, 119; academic field, 100

academic research group, 74

actor (actress), 26

address (form of), 26–7

administrators, 142

advocate, 59, 60; *see also* lawyer

agricultural household, 48, 96

America (contrast of Japan with), 6, 19, 32, 38, 48, 60, 73, 124, 126, 143, 147; American(s), 33, 44, 69, 73, 79, 85, 86, 93, 107, 116

American influence, 72

American occupation, 98

American style management, 85

American and British politics (contrasted with Japanese), 79

ancestor worship, 140

army, 44

artists, 59

Asahi Beer Company, 56

ba (location, frame), 1

bantō, 110

bars (taverns), 124–6

buraku, 20

bureaucracy, 88

bureaucratic: organ, 65; pattern, 37; stability, 46; structure, 51; system, 103, 142

Burma, 97

bushi, 141–42

business, 71

business enterprise, 14, 17; and firm, 93, 113; sector, 114

caste (Hindu), x, 2, 11, 21, 24, 39, 51, 82, 87, 88, 93, 101, 103, 104, 116; caste-consciousness, 88; caste-like, 112

central administration, 103; centralized administrative system, 115

child-companies, 93–4, 96, 110

China (contrasted with Japan), 24, 102, 142; Chinese, 21, 28–9, 137, 140; Chinese (family) system, 13; Chinese lineage, 129

chō-yō-no-jo, 28

civil code (post-war), 4

civil servant, 116–17

civil service, 114, 116, 119

class, x, 24, 28, 87, 93, 104

cliques (university), 112–13, 126, 145; political, 55

commander-in-chief, 67; commander and soldier, 71

company (companies), 25, 36, 38, 57, 58, 61, 69, 84, 85, 91, 92, 93

company houses, 10, 14, 16; company housing schemes, 18

consensus, group, 53, 57, 122, 144, 145; system, *see ringi-sei*

contract, 79–80; concept of, 77; contract system, 80; contractual arrangements, 15